# BIBLE STUDY on JOSEPH

## STUDENT WORKBOOK

### (For Older Children & Youth)

### Revised & Updated

by

Bisi Adeyi

Set Apart Child

BIBLE STUDY ON JOSEPH STUDENT WORKBOOK

(For Older Children & Youth)

Revised & Updated

Bible Study On Joseph Volume 2

Copyright © 2016, 2015 Bisi Adeyi

Published by Set Apart Child
Canada
www.setapartchild.com
Contact Email: setapartchild@gmail.com

ISBN: 978-1-988682-27-3

Images

Some of the images used in this book were purchased from Vector Stock and Graphics Factory but were modified by the author. The rest of the images were created by the author.

**Use for the glory of God**

# Table Of Content

For The Student: How To Use      4

Lesson 1: God's Word      6

Lesson 2: God's Love In The family      8

Lesson 3: God's Word And Dreams      12

Lesson 4: Temptation And Sin      16

Lesson 5: Serving Others      20

Lesson 6: Timing Of Events      24

Lesson 7: Gifts For God's Glory      28

Lesson 8: Guilt And Forgiveness      32

Lesson 9: Taking Responsibility      35

Lesson 10: Attitude To Suffering      39

Lesson 11: Love In Action      43

Lesson 12: Forgiving Others      46

Lesson 13: Submitting To God's Will      49

Lesson 14: Honouring Your Parents      53

Lesson 15: Faith In God      57

Lesson 16: God Turning Evil Into Good      60

Curriculums      65

About The Author      66

# For The Student: How To Use

**Using this Bible Study**

Take time to pray for the Holy Spirit's insight and believe God to use this Bible study to reveal Himself to you. Allow God to minister His Word to you and be committed to applying what He has taught you to in your life.

**Bible Study Format**

*BIBLE STUDY ON JOSEPH (For Older Children & Youth)* is a Bible study material designed to allow you to answer most of the questions in this workbook based on the Bible passages given.

**The Lessons**

Each lesson is based on an aspect of Joseph's life except for the first lesson. The first lesson is the introductory lesson on the importance of studying God's Word for knowledge and life application. The rest of the lessons are divided into two sections—a: Joseph's life and b: its life application. The sections *a* and *b* of each lesson may be studied together or separately.

**Memory Verses**

There are the only two memory verses for the entire *BIBLE STUDY ON JOSEPH (For Older Children & Youth)*. Do your best to memorise them.

**Main Bible Text**

Usually most of the Scriptures for the lesson study on Joseph's life are from the main Bible text but not limited to it. For this Kindle edition, links to the New International Version (NIV) of the text are provided.

**Topic**

The topic for each lesson indicates a theme from God's Word that is focused on in Joseph's life and its life application to you. The questions in the lesson are tailored toward this theme.

**Aim**

The aim for each section summarizes what is to be studied in Joseph's life or its application to your life based on the topic.

**Review**

The review helps to refresh your memory on the last lesson.

## Comments

These are background information and explanations provided where applicable to help you know more, understand the questions asked, and guide the answers expected.

Those comments that give away the answers to the questions before them have been moved to the end of the lesson. When you have finished answering those questions, take the time to read the comments before continuing with the rest of the study.

## Definitions

Where necessary, certain terms are defined to help you understand the context those terms are used in the lesson.

## Questions (and Answers)

Make sure to read every Scripture and use it to answer the corresponding question.

The intro questions in the life application sections enable you to ponder on or share your personal experiences. From the second lesson, the last questions in both sections *a* and *b* encourage you to articulate what you have learned from the lessons. As much as possible tailor your contributions/ answers to the aim of the section.

## Prayer

Take time to pray in rounding up the lesson. The prayers should not be limited to the prayer points given.

## Assignment

The assignment for each lesson is the main Bible text to read for the next lesson.

## Ground Rules in a Class or Group Setting

Below are suggested ground rules to adhere to:

- Be orderly in your contributions. Receive the leader's permission before you ask or answer questions, read the Scripture or give any contribution.
- Do not dominate the discussion. Allow others to participate.
- Do not make fun of any contribution. Respect each other's feelings.
- Feel free to ask questions. Remember, there are no dumb questions.
- Keep all personal experiences shared confidential. Do not look down on the sharer.

# Lesson 1: God's Word

**Memory Verses**

**Genesis 50:20** - You intended to harm me, but God intended it for good to accomplish what is now being done, the saving of many lives.

**Romans 8:28** - And we know that in all things God works for the good of those who love him, who have been called according to his purpose.

_____

**Main Bible Text: Matthew 7:24-27**

**Aim: In this lesson, you will do a study on the importance of studying God's Word for knowledge and life application.**

1. Read **2Timothy 3:16-17** - **All Scripture is God-breathed and is useful for teaching, rebuking, correcting and training in righteousness, so that the servant of God may be thoroughly equipped for every good work.**
a. Underline the 4 things that God's Word is useful for.

b. What is the result for you?

2. Read **Psalm 119:105.** What does it mean for God's Word to be:
a. "A lamp for my feet?"

b. "A light on my path?"

_____

3. Read **Romans 12:2 - Do not conform to the pattern of this world, but be transformed by the renewing of your mind. Then you will be able to test and approve what God's will is—his good, pleasing and perfect will.** Underline the 2 things you will be able to do concerning God's will when you study and renew your mind through His Word.

4. Read **Matthew 7:24-27**. What is the main difference between the wise and foolish builders concerning God's Word?

5. Read **James 1:22**. What you are to do with God's Word?

6. Read **James 1:25 - But whoever looks intently into the perfect law that gives freedom, and continues in it—not forgetting what they have heard, but doing it—they will be blessed in what they do.** Underline what happens to you when you hear and apply God's Word to your life by doing it

7. Read **Genesis 50:20** and **Romans 8:28**. From your <u>previous</u> knowledge about the life of Joseph:
a.   How do these two verses fit into Joseph's life?

b. How can you apply these verses to your own life?

_____

**Prayer**
1. Thank God for this Bible study material.
2. Pray that God will use your study on Joseph to help you know His Word better and mold you to be a better person.
3. Pray that God will help you to be faithful in studying His Word.

**Assignment**
Read **Genesis 35:22b-26** before the next lesson.

# Lesson 2: God's Love In The family

**Memory Verses**

Genesis 50:20 - You intended to harm me, but God intended it for good to accomplish what is now being done, the saving of many lives.

Romans 8:28 - And we know that in all things God works for the good of those who love him, who have been called according to his purpose.

Review: In the last lesson, the importance of studying God's Word for knowledge and life application was studied.

_____

## Section a: Joseph and His Family

**Main Bible Text: Genesis 35:22b-26**

Aim: In this section, you will do a study on the kind of relationship Joseph's family had with each other.

*Comment: Joseph's father, Jacob (also known as Israel), descended from Abraham whom God entered into covenant with. Abraham and his wife, Sarah, gave birth to Isaac. Jacob and Esau (his twin brother) were the children of Isaac and Rebecca.*

1. Read **Genesis 35:22b-26**. What were the names of Jacob's four wives?

*(See comment)*

2. Read each Bible verse below to find out:

a. the name of the son.

b. the meaning of his name (if your Bible has a footnote, use it).

c. the son's mother.

| Verse | a. Name | b. Meaning | c. Mother |
|---|---|---|---|
| **Genesis 29:32** | | | |
| **Genesis 29:33** | | | |
| **Genesis 29:34** | | | |
| **Genesis 29:35** | | | |
| **Genesis 30:4-6** | | | |
| **Genesis 30:7-8** | | | |
| **Genesis 30:9-11** | | | |
| **Genesis 30:12-13** | | | |
| **Genesis 30:17-18** | | | |
| **Genesis 30:19-20** | | | |
| **Genesis 30:22-24** | | | |
| **Genesis 35:16-18** | | | |

3. From your answers to #2 above, answer the following:

a. How many brothers did Joseph have?



b. What number was Joseph among his brothers?



4. From the meanings of Joseph's and his brothers' names, what kind of relationship do you think existed between his mother and his stepmothers?

5. Read **Genesis 30:19-21**. In addition to his brothers, Joseph had a sister.
a. What was his sister's name?


b. What was her mother's name?


6. Read **Genesis 37:2-4**. What kind of relationship did the following people have with Joseph:
a. His father?


b. His brothers?


7. What is the main thing you have learned about Joseph and his family?

_____

## Section b:  Life Application
**Aim: In this section, you will do a study on the kind of relationship God wants you to have within your family.**

Intro Question: What kind of relationship do you have with each member of your family?

1. Read the following Scriptures to find out the kind of relationship God expects between the following members of the family.

a. **Ephesians 6:1-2**. Children to parents.

b. **Ephesians 6:4**. Parents to children.

c. **Psalm 133:1**. Between brothers and sisters.

2. Read **1 John 4:7-11** and apply it to your family.

a. What kind of relationship should you have with every member of your family?

b. Why?

3. What have you learned about God's expectation for the relationship between you and your family?

_____

**Prayer**

1. Thank God for what you have learned about Joseph's family.
2. Thank God for every member of your family, mentioning each of them by name.
3. If you do NOT love EVERY member of your family, ask God to forgive you and help you to love them.

**Assignment**

Read **Genesis 37:1-11** before the next lesson.

*Comment: Leah and Rachel were sisters. Jacob loved and intended to marry Rachel, but as a result of a trick played on him by Laban (Rachel's father) he got married to Leah instead. Later, he married Rachel. Bilhah was Rachel's maid, while Zilpah was Leah's maid; and he ended up marrying both maids as well.*

## Lesson 3: God's Word And Dreams

**Memory Verses**

**Genesis 50:20 - You intended to harm me, but God intended it for good to accomplish what is now being done, the saving of many lives.**

**Romans 8:28 - And we know that in all things God works for the good of those who love him, who have been called according to his purpose.**

Review: In the last lesson, the kind of relationship Joseph's family had with each other and the kind of relationship God wants you to have in your own family were studied.

_____

## Section a: Joseph's Dreams

**Main Bible Text: Genesis 37:1-11**

**Aim: In this section, you will do a study on how God turned Joseph's dreams into reality.**

1. Read **Genesis 37:6-7, 9**.
a. What was Joseph's first dream?



b. What was his second dream?



2. Read **Genesis 37:8, 10**. What did both dreams mean?



3. Read **Genesis 37:5-11**. What feelings did the dream generate among Joseph's brothers towards him?

4. Read **Genesis 37:18-20, 26-28**. What actions did his brothers take to make sure Joseph's dreams did not become a reality?

*Comment: After 13 years, through God's intervention, Joseph became the second-in-command in Egypt. Due to famine, his brothers came to Egypt and came in contact with him but did not recognize him.*

5. Read the following Scriptures to find out how Joseph's dreams came to reality.
a. **Genesis 42:6-9**.

b. **Genesis 43:26-28**.

c. **Genesis 44:12-14**.

d. **Genesis 50:15, 18**.

e. **Genesis 48:21-22**.

*Comment: In addition, Joseph's dreams meant that he was going to take the position of the first son to be the leader of the family. Among the Israelites, the first son became the head of the family when the father died and received twice as much money and property as each of his brothers. Joseph's first dream also became a reality when Jacob adopted both Manasseh and Ephraim (Joseph's two sons) as his sons (Genesis 48:5). These two grandsons would each receive a full share along with Jacob's other eleven sons, and by doing this, Jacob gave Joseph's family a double share in the inheritance.*

6. What is the main thing you have learned about Joseph's dreams?

## Section b: Life Application
**Aim: In this section, you will do a study on the fulfillment of God's Word and dreams.**

Intro Question: Share a dream you had (or you wish you had) which you would like to become a reality?

1. Read **Job 33:14-18**.
a. **Job 33:14** - What does God do?

b. **Job 33:15** - When does God speak?

c. **Job 33:16–18** - Why does God sometimes speak through dreams?

2. Dreams
a. Read **Job 33:14**. Dreams may be because of?

b. Read **Ecclesiastes 5:3a**. Dreams may be because of?

c. Read **Isaiah 29:8**. Dreams may be because of?

*Comment: The Scripture refers to all or part of the Bible.*

3. Read **2Timothy 3:16**.
a. Who is the source of the Scripture?

b. What is another term apart from the "Bible" that refers to the Scripture?

4. Read and compare **2Timothy 3:16** with **Job 33:14-18**. In what ways is the Scripture similar to dreams?

5. Read and compare **2Peter 1:19-21** with **Ecclesiastes 5:3a**. How is the Scripture much better than dreams?

6. Read **Isaiah 55:11**. When God gives you His Word, what can you be sure of?

7. From the above study on dreams and God's Word, which one can you be COMPLETELY SURE will get fulfilled in your life - God's Word or dreams?

8. What have you learned about the fulfillment of God's Word and dreams for you?

_____

**Prayer**
1. Thank God that you can be completely sure about the fulfillment of His Word.
2. Thank God for His Word concerning you and the fulfillment of it.
3. Pray that God will reveal to you His Word concerning you.

**Assignment**
Read **Genesis 39:1-23** before the next lesson.

**Memory Verses**

**Genesis 50:20** - You intended to harm me, but God intended it for good to accomplish what is now being done, the saving of many lives.

**Romans 8:28** - And we know that in all things God works for the good of those who love him, who have been called according to his purpose.

Review: In the last lesson, how God turned Joseph's dreams into reality and the fulfillment of God's Word and dreams were studied.

_____

## Section a: Joseph Overcoming Temptation

**Main Bible Text: Genesis 39:1-23**

**Aim:** In this section, you will do a study on how Joseph overcame temptation in Potiphar's house.

*Definition: Sin is disobeying God's Word or doing what is wrong, while temptation is anything or anybody that can lead you to sin. Temptation is not sin; but it will lead to sin **if** you give in to it.*

1. Read **Genesis 39:6**. To what extend did Potiphar trust Joseph?

2. Read **Genesis 39:7**. What did Potiphar's wife ask Joseph to do?

_____

3. Read **Genesis 39:8-9**.

a. What was Joseph's response to Potiphar's wife's request?

b. Why did he have that response?

c. Who did he say he would sin against if he responded the way she wanted?

4. Read **Genesis 39:10**. For how long did Joseph maintain his response to Potiphar's wife's request?

5. Read **Genesis 39:11-12.**

a. What did Potiphar's wife do to Joseph?

b. What did he do in return?

6. Read **Genesis 39:13-18**. Was Potiphar's wife's account of what happened true?

7. Read **Genesis 39:19-20**. What did Potiphar do to Joseph?

8. Read **Genesis 39:20-21**. What did God do for Joseph where he was?

9. What did you learn about the temptation Joseph went through in Potiphar's house?

*(See comment)*

## Section b: Life Application

**Aim: In this section, you will do a study on how you can avoid sinning when you are tempted.**

Intro Question: Share about an experience you have had when you have been tempted to do something that was wrong but you did not do it?

1. Read **1Corinthians 10:13**.
a. What kinds of temptations will come your way?

b. Why would God not allow you to be tempted beyond what you can withstand?

c. When you are tempted, what has God promised to do?

**Fear of the Lord**
*Comment: Joseph did not give in to the temptation from Potiphar's wife and sin because he feared the Lord. (Genesis 39:9 - No one is greater in this house than I am. My master has withheld nothing from me except you, because you are his wife. How then could I do such a wicked thing and sin against God?)*

2. In each of the verses below, underline what the fear of the Lord does for you.
a. Read **Exodus 20:20 - Moses said to the people, "Do not be afraid. God has come to test you, so that the fear of God will be with you to keep you from sinning."**
b. Read **Proverbs 8:13 - To fear the Lord is to hate evil; I hate pride and arrogance, evil behavior and perverse speech.**
c. Read **Proverbs 16:6 - Through love and faithfulness sin is atoned for; through the fear of the Lord evil is avoided.**

3. In each of the verses below, how can you get the fear of the Lord?
a. Read **Psalm 34:11**.



b. Read **Jeremiah 32:40**.



c. Read **Psalm 86:11**.




4. Jesus our example: Read **Hebrews 4:15**.
a. In how many ways was Jesus tempted?



b. Did he give in to the temptation to sin?



5. Read **Hebrews 4:16**. How do you receive help not to give in to the temptation to sin?




6. What have you learned from God's Word about how you can overcome temptation and not sin?




_____

**Prayer**
1. Thank God for the study you have done on how Joseph overcame temptation.
2. Pray that God will help you to apply what you have learned on Joseph in your own life.
3. Pray that the fear of the Lord will increase in your heart.
4. Pray that God will help you to ask for His help anytime you are tempted so that you will not sin.

**Assignment**
Read **Genesis 39:20-40:23** before the next lesson.

*Comment: From the study above, Potiphar's wife asking Joseph to sleep with her was not a sin to him but a temptation. It would have become a sin to Joseph if he gave in to the temptation by sleeping with her. Realize that temptation will always come, but you do not have to give in to it and sin.*

**Memory Verses**

Genesis 50:20 - You intended to harm me, but God intended it for good to accomplish what is now being done, the saving of many lives.

Romans 8:28 - And we know that in all things God works for the good of those who love him, who have been called according to his purpose.

Review: In the last lesson, how Joseph overcame temptation in Potiphar's house and how you can avoid sinning when you are tempted were studied.

_____

## Section a: Joseph And Service
**Main Bible Text: Genesis 39:20-40:23**

Aim: In this section, you will do a study on how Joseph served others in different situations.

1. Read **Genesis 37:12-17.**

a. What service did Jacob ask Joseph to do for him?

b. Where did Jacob say Joseph would find his brothers?

c. When Joseph got there, did he find his brothers?

d. Where was he told he would find them?

e. What did Joseph do when he was told his brothers were in another place?

*(See comment)*

_____

2. Read **Genesis 39:2-6.**
a. What did Potiphar put Joseph in charge of?

b. How do you think Joseph served Potiphar even though he was a slave?

3. Read **Genesis 39:20-23.**
a. What did the prison warden put Joseph in charge of?

b. How do you think Joseph did his job in prison even though he was put in prison unjustly?

4. Read **Genesis 40:1-8**.
a. Who were the two people assigned to Joseph in the prison?

b. When Joseph saw them looking sad, what did he do?

c. Why were the two people sad?

d. What did Joseph offer to do for them?

5. What have you learned about how Joseph served others in different situations in his life?

## Section b: Life Application

**Aim: In this section, you will do a study on how God expects you to serve others.**

Intro Question: Share about a service you have done or you do for others over a period of time either at home, in school, in church, or in the community.

1. Read **Ephesians 6:7**. When you are serving others, whom are you actually serving?

2. In each of the verses below, how should you serve others?
a. Read **Ephesians 6:7**.

b. Read **Galatians 5:13b**.

3. Read **Galatians 6:10**. From the following choices below, what should determine your service to others? *The way I feel | The opportunity | Others' reaction*

4. Read **Galatians 6:9.**

a. What is God's instruction about continuing to serve others?

b. What happens when you continue to serve others?

5. What have you learned about how God expects you to serve others?

---

**Prayer**

1. Thank God for the study on Joseph and service.
2. Pray that God will grant you the grace to serve others from your heart always.

**Assignment**

Read **Genesis 41:1-14** before the next lesson.

*Comment: Joseph was sent by his father to find out if all was well with his brothers. On getting there, he found out that his brothers had moved on. He did not give up and go back home, but he continued to look for them even though that meant more work for him.*

# Lesson 6: Timing Of Events

**Memory Verses**

**Genesis 50:20** - You intended to harm me, but God intended it for good to accomplish what is now being done, the saving of many lives.

**Romans 8:28** - And we know that in all things God works for the good of those who love him, who have been called according to his purpose.

**Review:** In the last lesson, how Joseph served others in different situations and how God expects you to serve others were studied.

## Section a: Timing Of Events In Joseph's Life

**Main Bible Text: Genesis 41:1-14**

**Aim:** In this section, you will do a study on how God determined the timing of events in Joseph's life.

1. Read **Genesis 40:9-11**. What was the chief cupbearer's dream about?




2. Read **Genesis 40:12-13**. What interpretation did Joseph give to the dream?




3. Read **Genesis 40:12.** In how many days will the dream be fulfilled?

4. Read **Genesis 40:14.** What was Joseph's request to the chief cupbearer?

5. Read **Genesis 40:23.** What did the chief cupbearer do about Joseph's request?

6. Read **Genesis 41:8-14.** How did Pharaoh get to hear about Joseph?

7. Read **Genesis 41:1.** How many years had passed before the chief cupbearer mentioned Joseph to Pharaoh?

8. Read **Genesis 37:2.** How old was Joseph when he had those two dreams?

9. Read **Genesis 41:46.** How old was Joseph when he became the second-in-command of Egypt?

10. How many years did it take for Joseph's dreams to be fulfilled?

*(See comment)*

11. What have you learned about God's timing of events in Joseph's life?

<u>**Section b: Life Application**</u>
**Aim: In this section, you will do a study on how God holds the timing of events in your life in His hand.**

Intro Question: Have you ever had to wait a long time before getting something that was promised to you? Or do you know of anyone that was given a promise and had to wait a long time before it happened? Share either one.

1. Read **Ecclesiastes 3:1.** What is there for everything?

2. Read **Ecclesiastes 3:11.**
a. Who determines the time for everything?

b. When does God make everything beautiful?

*Comment: God told Habakkuk about an event or revelation that would happen at a certain time in the future.*

3. Read **Habakkuk 2:3.**
a. What did God tell Habakkuk to do if the revelation seemed to linger?

b. Why?

4. Read **Jeremiah 1:12**. What does God do to make sure that His Word gets fulfilled?

5. What have you learned about God's timing of events in your own life?

---

**Prayer**
1. Thank God for the study on the timing of events in Joseph's life.
2. Thank God that your life and all the events of your life are in His hands.
3. Pray that God will grant you the grace to wait for Him to work things out in your life in His time.

**Assignment**
Read **Genesis 41:15-57** before the next lesson.

**Comment:** *After interpreting the chief cupbearer's dream, Joseph told him to tell Pharaoh about him as soon as he got out. Probably if that had happened, Joseph might have been released, gone back home and would not have been around to interpret Pharaoh's dreams. But God had greater plans for him to become the second-in-command of Egypt by interpreting Pharaoh's dreams.*
*As a boy, Joseph had 2 dreams which meant that his brothers would bow to him. These dreams were fulfilled when he became the second-in-command of Egypt.*

# Lesson 7: Gifts For God's Glory

**Memory Verses**

**Genesis 50:20** - You intended to harm me, but God intended it for good to accomplish what is now being done, the saving of many lives.

**Romans 8:28** - And we know that in all things God works for the good of those who love him, who have been called according to his purpose.

**Review:** In the last lesson, how God determined the timing of events in Joseph's life and how God holds the timing of events in your life in His hand were studied.

## Section a: Joseph And The Interpretation Of Dreams

**Main Bible Text: Genesis 41:15-57**

**Aim:** In this section, you will do a study on how Joseph gave glory to God for his gift of interpretation of dreams.

***Definition:*** *Gifts, in this context, refer to the abilities and talents you possess. To give glory to God for your gifts is to acknowledge Him as the One who gave you (or made it possible for you to possess) those abilities and talents and, as such, give Him praise for them.*

***Comment:*** *Pharaoh had two dreams which no one could interpret for him. Then the chief cupbearer remembered that Joseph could interpret dreams and he mentioned this to Pharaoh. Pharaoh had Joseph brought before him.*

1. Read **Genesis 41:15.** What did Pharaoh hear about Joseph?

2. Read **Genesis 41:16.** Who did Joseph say would interpret the dreams?

3. Read **Genesis 41:17-21.** What was Pharaoh's first dream?

4. Read **Genesis 41:22-24.** What was Pharaoh's second dream?

5, Read **Genesis 42:26-27.** What did the two dreams mean?

6. Read **Genesis 41:25.** How many interpretations did Joseph give to the two dreams?

7. Read **Genesis 41:32.** Why?

8. Read **Genesis 41:39.** Who did Pharaoh say had made known the interpretation of the dreams to Joseph?

9. Read **Genesis 41:40.** What happened to Joseph because he interpreted Pharaoh's dreams?

10. What have you learned about Joseph giving glory to God for his ability to interpret dreams?

## Section b: Life Application

**Aim: In this section, you will do a study on how you should give glory to God for your gifts**

Intro Question: Share how you have used one of your talents and abilities to help other people.

1. Read **Romans 12:6.** What kinds of gifts (talents and abilities) does each person have?

2. Read **Ephesians 4:7-8.** Who has given you your gifts?

3. God told the Israelites how He would bless them in the Promised Land. Read **Deuteronomy 8:17-18.**
a. What did God say the Israelites might say to themselves?

b. Would what they might say be true?

c. What has God done for them?

d. How are they to acknowledge what God did for them?

4. Read **1Corinthians 10:31.** What are you to do for the glory of God?

5. Read **Isaiah 42:8.** What will God not give to another?

6. Read **Acts 12:21-23.**
a. What ability did Herod display?

b. Why was Herod struck down?

7. Based on the Bible passages above, how can you give God the glory for your talents and abilities?

8. What have you learned about giving God the glory for your talents and abilities?

---

**Prayer**
1. Thank God for all the gifts (talents and abilities) He has blessed you with.
2. Pray that He will help you to always give Him the glory for your gifts.

**Assignment**
Read **Genesis 42:1-38** before the next lesson.

# Lesson 8: Guilt And Forgiveness

**Memory Verses**

Genesis 50:20 - You intended to harm me, but God intended it for good to accomplish what is now being done, the saving of many lives.

Romans 8:28 - And we know that in all things God works for the good of those who love him, who have been called according to his purpose.

**Review:** In the last lesson, how Joseph gave glory to God for his gift of interpretation of dreams and how you should give glory to God for your gifts were studied.

_____

## Section a: Joseph's Brothers' Guilt And Forgiveness

**Main Bible Text: Genesis 42:1-38**

**Aim:** In this section, you will do a study on how Joseph's brothers dealt with their guilt through forgiveness.

*Comment: As predicted, famine spread over the world after seven years of plenty. Back in Canaan, Joseph's family too was affected by the famine. On learning that there was grain in Egypt, Jacob sent his sons except Benjamin to buy grain. Joseph had become the second-in-command at this time and his brothers did not recognize him for two reasons. First, they sold him into slavery, so they never expected him to be the second-in-command of Egypt. Second, the Egyptians dressed very differently from the Jews and Joseph must have been dressed as an Egyptian. Joseph, however, recognized them but decided to test them to see what kind of men they had become. So he made up a story that they were spies and threatened to punish them.*

1. Read **Genesis 42:21-22.**

a. What did Joseph's brothers say was the reason they were being punished?

b. Why did they feel guilty about the reason?

2. Read **Genesis 37:31-33.** When Joseph's brothers sold him into slavery many years ago, what did they lead their father to believe?


3. Read **Genesis 42:13**. When Joseph's brothers were talking to him, what did they tell him happened to their brother, Joseph?


4. Read **Genesis 42:38.** Despite their feeling guilty, did Joseph's brothers tell Jacob the truth about what they had done to Joseph?

*Comment: Much later, Joseph revealed his identity to his brothers and he brought his whole family down to Egypt to live. After the death of Jacob, Joseph's brothers sent a message to him.*

5. Read **Genesis 50:15.** Why did Joseph's brothers feel that he might still punish them for what they did to him?


6. Read **Genesis 50:16-17.** What did Joseph's brothers ask him to do to them?


7. Read **Genesis 50:19-21.**
a. What was Joseph's response to his brothers' request?


b. Why?


8. What have you learned about how Joseph's brothers dealt with their guilt through forgiveness?

## Section b: Life Application
**Aim: In this section, you will do a study on how you should deal with guilt through forgiveness**

Intro Question: Have you ever done something bad to someone that you did not apologize to him or her IMMEDIATELY? Share it.

1. Read **Proverbs 28:13a**. What happens when you hide your sins and do not confess them?

2. Read **Luke 15:21.** The prodigal son sinned against his father by asking for his inheritance at the wrong time and wasting it. In asking for forgiveness, whom did he say he had sinned against apart from his father?

3. Read **1John 1:9.** What happens when you confess your sins?

4. Read **Proverbs 28:13b.** What happens when you confess your sins?

5. Read **Matthew 5:23-24.** How important is asking for forgiveness?

6. What have you learned from God's Word about why you need to ask for forgiveness when you are guilty of wrongdoing?

**Prayer**
1. Thank God for what you have learned on dealing with guilt through forgiveness.
2. Pray that God will grant you the grace to forgive as Joseph did.
3. Ask God for the grace to always ask for forgiveness from Him and the persons you have wronged.

**Assignment**
Read **Genesis 44:17-34** before the next lesson.

# Lesson 9: Taking Responsibility

**Memory Verses**

Genesis 50:20 - You intended to harm me, but God intended it for good to accomplish what is now being done, the saving of many lives.

Romans 8:28 - And we know that in all things God works for the good of those who love him, who have been called according to his purpose.

Review: In the last lesson, how Joseph's brothers dealt with their guilt through forgiveness and how you should deal with guilt through forgiveness were studied.

## Section a: Joseph's Brothers And Responsibility
Main Bible Text: Genesis 44:17-34

**Aim:** In this lesson, you will do a study on how Joseph's brothers took responsibility

*Definition: Taking responsibility is taking up a duty, job or service to complete it and being willing to accept the credit (good or bad) for the outcome.*

*Comment: Joseph accused his brothers of being spies. To prove their innocence, they told him about their family—revealing they had a younger brother, Benjamin, at home. To test them, Joseph asked his brothers to bring Benjamin to him.*

1. Read **Genesis 42:37.**

a. What responsibility did Reuben want to undertake?

b. What did Reuben tell his father to do to him if he failed?

2. Read **Genesis 42:38.** Did Jacob agree?

3. Read **Genesis 43:8-9.**

a. What responsibility did Judah want to undertake?




b. What did Judah tell his father to do to him if he failed?




4. Read **Genesis 43:11-14.** Did Jacob agree?




*(See comment)*


5. Read **Genesis 44:18.** Who spoke up to defend Benjamin?




6. Read **Genesis 44:18-34.** After recounting the story of his taking responsibility, what did Judah plead with Joseph to do?




**Comment:** *Joseph was so deeply moved by the speech that he revealed himself to his brothers. He sent them back with lots of goods and carts to bring back their entire family. Benjamin returned back with them. Thereby, Joseph's brother fulfilled his responsibility to his father.*




7. What have you learned about the way Joseph's brother handled his responsibility?

## Section b: Life Application

**Aim: In this lesson, you will do a study on the importance of taking responsibility.**

Intro Question: Share about a big job you were given to do and how you did it?

1. Read **1Corinthians 4:2.** When you are given something to do (a trust), what is required of you?

2. Read **Luke 16:10.** When you are given a little responsibility and you do it well, what will happen?

3. Read **Luke 19:12-13.** What responsibilities did the master give his servants?

4. Read **Luke 19:16-17.**
a. How well did this servant do with his responsibility?

b. What was his reward?

5. Read **Luke 19:20-24.**
a. How well did this servant do with his responsibility?

b. What was his reward?

6. Compare **1Corinthians 15:58** with **Ephesians 6:7-8.**

a. How are you to do God's work or any other responsibility you are given?

b. Why?

7. What have you learned about how God expects you to handle responsibilities given to you?

---

**Prayer**

1. Thank God for what you have learned about taking responsibility.
2. Pray that God will help you be a person of fine character and take your responsibilities seriously.
3. Ask God to always be faithful with whatever responsibility you are given to do.

**Assignment**

Read **Genesis 45:1-11** before the next lesson.

*Comment: Note the difference in Reuben's and Judah's vows about bringing back Benjamin. Judah's vow was much lighter and yet Jacob released Benjamin to him. It is possible that Jacob did not trust Reuben because he had slept with Jacob's wife in the past (**Genesis 35:22**). Sometimes, a person's character determines whether or not he is given a responsibility. So Judah took Benjamin along with them on their journey back to Egypt so that Joseph could verify their story.*

*On his brothers' departure from Egypt, Joseph played a trick on them by putting his silver cup in Benjamin's sack. Then he sent his servants to accuse them of theft and search their sacks. Of course, the silver cup was found in Benjamin's sack. As a result, Joseph threatened to make Benjamin his slave.*

---

# Lesson 10: Attitude To Suffering

**Memory Verses**

**Genesis 50:20** - You intended to harm me, but God intended it for good to accomplish what is now being done, the saving of many lives.

**Romans 8:28** - And we know that in all things God works for the good of those who love him, who have been called according to his purpose.

**Review:** In the last lesson, how Joseph's brothers took responsibility and the importance of taking responsibility were studied.

## Section a: Joseph Attitude To Suffering

**Main Bible Text: Genesis 45:1-11**

**Aim:** In this section, you will do a study on Joseph's attitude to suffering for doing right.

*Comment: In Potiphar's house, his wife wanted Joseph to sleep with her. When Joseph refused, she lied against him. Potiphar believed his wife and threw Joseph into prison.*

1. Read **Genesis 39:20-23, 40:1-8.** What do you think Joseph's attitude was like in the prison?

2. Read **Genesis 39:20-23.** What did God do for Joseph in prison?

*Comment: For thirteen years, Joseph was a slave in Potiphar's house and then became a prisoner unjustly. But through God intervention, he ended up as the second-in-command in Egypt.*

3. Read **Genesis 42:21.** How did his brothers say Joseph felt when he was being sold as a slave?

4. Read **Genesis 40:15.** What did Joseph say about his being in Egypt while he was in prison?

5. Read **Genesis 50:20**. What did Joseph say his brothers thought they were doing to him?

6. Read **Genesis 45:5-8.** How did Joseph see his being sold into slavery?

7. What have you learned about Joseph's attitude to suffering for doing right?

---

## Section b: Life Application

**Aim: In this section, you will do a study on how God wants you to respond to suffering for doing right.**

Intro Question: Share about an experience you have had (or imagine) on suffering or being punished for doing what is right?

---

1. Read **Romans 8:28.** What does God do in ALL things for those who love Him?

2. Read **1Peter 3:17.** What should you be willing to suffer for?

3. Read **1Peter 4:15.** What should you NOT be willing to suffer for?

4. Underline what you should do when you suffer:

a. **1Peter 2:20b. - … But if you suffer for doing good and you endure it, this is commendable before God.**

b. **1Peter 4:16 - However, if you suffer as a Christian, do not be ashamed, but praise God that you bear that name.**

c. **James 1:2 - Consider it pure joy, my brothers and sisters, whenever you face trials of many kinds.**

5. Underline why you should endure suffering for doing the right thing:

a. **1Peter 2:21 - To this you were called, because Christ suffered for you, leaving you an example, that you should follow in his steps.**

b. **James 1:2-3 - Consider it pure joy, my brothers and sisters, whenever you face trials of many kinds, because you know that the testing of your faith produces perseverance.**

6. Underline what the end result is for suffering for doing what is right:

a. **1Peter 3:14 - But even if you should suffer for what is right, you are blessed. "Do not fear their threats; do not be frightened."**

b. **James 1:2-4 - Consider it pure joy, my brothers and sisters, whenever you face trials of many kinds, because you know that the testing of your faith produces perseverance. Let perseverance finish its work so that you may be mature and complete, not lacking anything.**

7. Read **Hebrews 13:5b.** What is God's promise to you even when you are going through suffering?

8. Read **Hebrews 13:6.** What should be your attitude to suffering?

9. What have you learned from God's Word about suffering for doing right and your attitude to it?

---

**Prayer**

1. Thank God that He brings about good in every situation.
2. Pray that you will have Joseph's kind of attitude to suffering for doing right.
3. Pray that God will grant you the grace to trust Him and have a positive attitude to suffering for doing right.

**Assignment**

Read **Genesis 47:1-12** before the next lesson.

# Lesson 11: Love In Action

**Memory Verses**

**Genesis 50:20** - You intended to harm me, but God intended it for good to accomplish what is now being done, the saving of many lives.

**Romans 8:28** - And we know that in all things God works for the good of those who love him, who have been called according to his purpose.

**Review:** In the last lesson, Joseph's attitude to suffering for doing right and how God wants you to respond to suffering for doing right were studied.

_____

## Section a: Joseph Showed Love To His Brothers
**Main Bible Text: Genesis 47:1-12**

**Aim:** In this section, you will do a study on how Joseph showed love to his brothers.

*Comment: After many years, Joseph was re-united with his brothers. He asked them to come to Egypt to live with their families so they would survive the famine.*

1. Read **Genesis 46:31.** Who did Joseph say he would speak to concerning his brothers?

2. Read **Genesis 46:31-32.** What would Joseph speak about?

3. Read **Genesis 46:33.** What did Joseph say his brothers would be asked?

4. Read **Genesis 46:34.** How were Joseph's brothers to answer?

5. Read **Genesis 47:11-12.**

a. Where did Joseph settle his brothers?

b. How was that place compared to the rest of Egypt?

c. What did he also do for them?

6. Why do you think Joseph did all these good things for his brothers?

7. What have you learned about how Joseph showed his love to his brothers?

_____

## Section b: Life Application

**Aim: In this section, you will do a study on how you should love others by what you do.**

Intro Question: Have you ever gone out of your way to do something good for someone else? Share it.

1. Read **Luke 10:27**. What is God's command to you about others?

2. Read **Romans 12:10** and **Galatians 5:13**. What is the common thing between these two verses?

3. **1Corinthians 13:5 - …[love] is not self-seeking…** What does this verse mean?

4. Read **1John 4:11**. Why are you to love others?

5. Read **1John 3:16**. What is love as Jesus showed it?

6. Read **1John 3:17**. How can love be shown in this case?

7. Read **1John 3:18**. How are you to love?

8. What have you learned about the way God wants you to show love to others?

---

**Prayer**
1. Thank God for what you have learned about showing love to others through Joseph's actions.
2. Pray that God will help you to show love to others in words and actions.
3. Pray that God will help you to love others even as He loves you.

**Assignment**
Read **Genesis 50:15-21** before the next lesson.

# Lesson 12: Forgiving Others

**Memory Verses**

**Genesis 50:20** - You intended to harm me, but God intended it for good to accomplish what is now being done, the saving of many lives.

**Romans 8:28** - And we know that in all things God works for the good of those who love him, who have been called according to his purpose.

**Review:** In the last lesson, how Joseph showed love to his brothers and how you should love others by what you do were studied.

## Section a: Joseph Forgave His Brothers

**Main Bible Text: Genesis 50:15-21**

**Aim: In this section, you will do a study on how Joseph forgave his brothers.**

*Comment: Even though his brothers sold him into slavery many years ago, Joseph made up with them and provided for them. After the death of their father, Joseph's brothers sent a message to him.*

1. Read **Genesis 50:15-17**.

a. What did Joseph's brothers ask him for?

b. Why?

c. What was Joseph's immediate reaction?

d. Why do you think Joseph had that reaction?

2. Read **Genesis 50:18**. What did his brothers offer to be to Joseph?

3. Read **Genesis 50:19.** Did Joseph accept?

4. Read **Genesis 50:20-21.** What did Joseph say he would do for his brothers?

5. How do you think Joseph showed that he forgave his brothers?

6. What have you learned about Joseph forgiving his brothers?

## Section b: Life Application

**Aim: In this section, you will do a study on how you should forgive others.**

Intro Question: Have anyone ever done something painful to you? Share it.

1. Read **Mathew 18: 23-25.** What did the servant do to the master?

2. Read **Mathew 18:26.** What did the servant say to the master?

3. Read **Mathew 18:27.** What was the master's response?

4. Read **Mathew 18:28.** What did one of his fellow servant do to the servant?

5. Read **Mathew 18:29.** What did the fellow servant say to the servant?

6. Read **Mathew 18:30.** What was the servant's response?

7. Read **Mathew 18:31-34.**

a. When the master heard what happened, what did he do?

b. Why?

8. **Ephesians 4:32 - Be kind and compassionate to one another, forgiving each other, just as in Christ God forgave you.** Underline why you should forgive others.

9. **Mathew 18:35 - "This is how my heavenly Father will treat each of you unless you forgive your brother or sister from your heart."** Underline how you should forgive others.

10. **Mathew 6:14 - For if you forgive other people when they sin against you, your heavenly Father will also forgive you.** Underline what happens when you forgive others.

11. **Mathew 6:15 - But if you do not forgive others their sins, your Father will not forgive your sins.** Underline what happens when you do NOT forgive others.

12. What have you learned from God's Word about how you should forgive others?

---

**Prayer**
1. Thank God for what you have learned about forgiving others.
2. Ask God to help you forgive others at all times.

**Assignment**
Read **Genesis 48:1-22** before the next lesson.

**Memory Verses**

**Genesis 50:20** - You intended to harm me, but God intended it for good to accomplish what is now being done, the saving of many lives.

**Romans 8:28** - And we know that in all things God works for the good of those who love him, who have been called according to his purpose.

Review: In the last lesson, how Joseph forgave his brothers and how you should forgive others were studied.

---

## Section a: Joseph Submitted To God's Will
**Main Bible Text: Genesis 48:1-22**

Aim: In this section, you will do a study on how Joseph submitted to and did God's will for his sons.

1. Read **Genesis 41:50.** How many sons did Joseph have?

2. Read **Genesis 41:51.**
a. What was the name of Joseph's first son?

b. What was the meaning of his name?

3. Read **Genesis 41:52.**
a. What was the name of Joseph's second son?

b. What was the meaning of his name?

4. Read **Genesis 48:8-9.** What did Joseph say about his sons in reply to Jacob's question?

*Comment: In the Jewish culture, when it comes to blessing, the right hand is very significant. When blessing two people at the same time, the right hand is for the older, while the left hand is for the younger.*

Read **Genesis 48:13.**
a. Who did Joseph intend for Jacob to put his right hand on?

b. Who did Joseph intend for Jacob to put his left hand on?

6. Read **Genesis 48:14.** What did Jacob do?

7. Read **Genesis 48:17-18.** Why was Joseph displeased about Jacob's action?

8. Read **Genesis 48:19.** What was Jacob's explanation?

9. Read **Genesis 48:19-20.** Did Joseph object after this?

10. Based on the above Bible passages, how do you think Joseph submitted to and did God's will for his sons?

11. What have you learned about how Joseph submitted to God's will for his sons?

---

## Section b: Life Application
**Aim: In this section, you will do a study on how to submit to and do God's will for your life.**

Intro Question: Have you ever being in a situation where your parent or teacher insisted you did something that was right even though you did not feel like doing it? Share it.

1. Read **Matthew 6:10**. What does God want concerning His will?

2. Read **Ephesians 5:17**. What does God want you to do concerning His will?

3. Read **Romans 12:2.** How do you know about God's will?

4. Read **Philippians 2:13.** What does God help you to do concerning His will?

5. Underline what kind of prayer you should pray about submitting to and doing God's will:
**Psalm 143:10 - Teach me to do your will, for you are my God; may your good Spirit lead me on level ground.**
**Matthew 26:39 - Going a little farther, he fell with his face to the ground and prayed, "My Father, if it is possible, may this cup be taken from me. Yet not as I will, but as you will."**
**James 4:15 - Instead, you ought to say, "If it is the Lord's will, we will live and do this or that."**

6. What have you learned from God's Word about submitting to and doing His will for your life?

_____

**Prayer**
1. Thank God for His will for your life.
2. Pray about submitting to and doing God's will for your life using the Bible verses under #5 above.

**Assignment**
Read **Genesis 49:29-50:14** before the next lesson.

# Lesson 14: Honouring Your Parents

**Memory Verses**

**Genesis 50:20** - You intended to harm me, but God intended it for good to accomplish what is now being done, the saving of many lives.

**Romans 8:28** - And we know that in all things God works for the good of those who love him, who have been called according to his purpose.

**Review:** In the last lesson, how Joseph submitted to and did God's will for his sons and how to submit to and do God's will for your life were studied.

## Section a: Joseph Honoured His Father

**Main Bible Text: Genesis 49:29-50:14**

**Aim: In this section, you will do a study on the various ways Joseph honoured his father.**

*Definition: To honour your parents is to have great respect and admiration for them. Also, you honour your parents by obeying them.*

1. Joseph honoured his father as a boy at home:

a. Read **Genesis 37:12-14.** What did Jacob tell Joseph to do?

b. Read **Genesis 37:15-17.** How did Joseph honour his father?

2. Read **Genesis 47:7.** Joseph honoured his father in Egypt:

a. What did Joseph do to his father?

b. How did Joseph honour his father?

3. Joseph honoured his father during the blessing of his sons:

a. Read **Genesis 48:17-18.** When Jacob placed his right hand on Ephraim, what did Joseph do initially?

b. Read **Genesis 48:19-20.** When Jacob insisted, did Joseph protest again?

c. How did Joseph honour his father?

4. Joseph honoured his father concerning burial instructions:

a. Read **Genesis 49:29-32.** What instruction did Jacob give concerning his burial?

b. Read **Genesis 50:4-5.** What was Joseph's request to Pharaoh?

c. Read **Genesis 50:12-14.** What did Joseph do about his father's instructions?

d. How did Joseph honour his father?

5. What have you learned about the various ways Joseph honoured his father?

## Section b: Life Application
**Aim: In this section, you will do a study on how you should honour your parents.**

Intro Question: In what ways can you honour your parents?

1. Read **Luke 2:48-51**.
a. What did Mary say they had been doing concerning Jesus?

b. What did Jesus say He was doing?

c. What did Jesus do by going with His parents to Nazareth?

2. Underline God's instruction to you about your parents.
a. **Exodus 20:12 - Honor your father and your mother, so that you may live long in the land the LORD your God is giving you.**
b. **Proverbs 1:8 - Listen, my son, to your father's instruction and do not forsake your mother's teaching.**
c. **Ephesians 6:1- Children, obey your parents in the Lord, for this is right.**

3. Why should you honour (obey) your parents?

a. Read **Ephesians 6:1**.

b. Read **Colossians 3:20**.

4. Read **Ephesians 6:2-3**. What is the promise that comes from honouring your parents?

5. What have you learned about God's instructions on honouring your parents?

---

**Prayer**

1. Thank God for your parents.
2. Thank God for what you have learned about the various ways to honour your parents.
3. Pray that God will help you to honour your parents in all you do.

**Assignment**

Read **Genesis 50:22-26** before the next lesson.

**Faith in God**

**Memory Verses**

Genesis 50:20 - You intended to harm me, but God intended it for good to accomplish what is now being done, the saving of many lives.

Romans 8:28 - And we know that in all things God works for the good of those who love him, who have been called according to his purpose.

Review: In the last lesson, the various ways Joseph honoured his father and how you should honour your parents were studied.

_____

## Section a: Joseph's Last Days

**Main Bible Text: Genesis 50:22-26**

Aim: In this section, you will do a study on Joseph's faith in God about his future.

1. Read **Genesis 50:24.** When Joseph was dying, what did he say God was going to do for the children of Israel?

2. Read **Genesis 50:25**. What did he make his brothers promise?

3. Read **Genesis 50:26.**

a. How old was Joseph when he died?

b. Where was he buried?

*Comment: About 400 years later, God fulfilled His promise and brought the Israelites out of Egypt with Moses as their leader.*

4. Read **Exodus 13:18-19**.
a. What did Moses do about the bones of Joseph?

b. Why did Moses take the bones?

*Comment: The Israelites spent 40 years in the wilderness before they got to Canaan – the Promised Land. Joshua was their leader at this time.*

5. Read **Joshua 24:32**. Where were Joseph's bones buried?

6. Read **Hebrews 11:22**. How did Joseph know that his instructions about his burial would be carried out?

7. What have you learned about Joseph's faith in God for his future?

---

## Section b: Life Application
**Aim: In this section, you will do a study on how you should have faith in God about your future.**

Intro Question: Share a specific thing you would like to happen to you in future?

1. Read **Matthew 6:25, 34.** What is God telling you about your future?

2. Read **Jeremiah 29:11**. What kind of plans does God have for your future?

3. Read **Matthew 6:33**. What should you concentrate on concerning your future?

4. Read **Philippians 1:6.**
a. What has God begun in you?

b. What is the end result?

5. Read **1Corinthians 1:8-9.**
a. What will God do about your future?

b. Why?

6. What have you learned from God's Word about faith in Him for your future?

_____

**Prayer**
1. Thank God that your future is in His hand.
2. Thank God for His faithfulness in ensuring a good future for you.
3. Pray that God will help you have the kind of faith that Joseph had in God for his future.

**Assignment**
Read **Genesis 50:20; Romans 8:28** before the next lesson.

# Lesson 16: God Turning Evil Into Good

**Memory Verses**

Genesis 50:20 - You intended to harm me, but God intended it for good to accomplish what is now being done, the saving of many lives.

Romans 8:28 - And we know that in all things God works for the good of those who love him, who have been called according to his purpose.

Review: In the last lesson, Joseph's faith in God about his future and how you should have faith in God about your future were studied.

_____

## Section a: Joseph's Life

**Main Bible Text: Genesis 50:20; Romans 8:28.**

Aim: In this section, you will do a concluding study on how God turned evil into good in Joseph's life.

Discuss how God turned evil into good in Joseph's life in the following instances:

1. Read **Genesis 37:19-28.**

2. Read **Genesis 39:1-6.**

3. Read **Genesis 39:20-23.**

4. Read **Genesis 41:1-14.**

5. Read **Genesis 41:37-45.**

6. Read **Genesis 41:50-52.**

7. Read **Genesis 37:5-11, 42:6, 43:26-28, 44:14, 50:18.**

8. Read **Genesis 37:5-8, 48:5, 20-22.**

9. Read **Genesis 50:19-20.**

10. What have you learned about how God turned evil into good in Joseph's life?

## Section b: Life Application
**Aim: In this section, you will do a study on how God will turn evil into good in your life.**

Intro Question: Have you ever had a bad experience that turned out later to be good after all? Share it.

1. Read **Romans 8:28.** What will God do for you?

2. Read **Romans 8:32.**
a. What has God done for you?

b. As a result of that, what will He do for you?

3. Read **Romans 8:34.**
a. What has Jesus done for you?

b. What is He doing for you now?

4. **Romans 8:35-39 - Who shall separate us from the love of Christ? Shall trouble or hardship or persecution or famine or nakedness or danger or sword? As it is written: "For your sake we face death all day long; we are considered as sheep to be slaughtered." No, in all these things we are more than conquerors through him who loved us. For I am convinced that neither death nor life, neither angels nor demons, neither the present nor the future, nor any powers, neither height nor depth, nor anything else in all creation, will be able to separate us from the love of God that is in Christ Jesus our Lord.** Underline all the things mentioned that CANNOT separate you from the love of God in Christ.

5. **Romans 8:31 - What, then, shall we say in response to these things? If God is for us, who can be against us?** Based on #4, what is the answer to this verse?

6. **Genesis 50:20 - You intended to harm me, but God intended it for good to accomplish what is now being done, the saving of many lives.**
**Romans 8:28 - And we know that in all things God works for the good of those who love him, who have been called according to his purpose.** From your study on the life of Joseph:
a. How do these two verses fit into Joseph's life?

b. How can you now apply them to your own life?

7. Based on **Romans 8:28-39**, what is the guarantee that God will **always** turn any evil into good in your life?
*Change the numbers into letters to find out (Clue – 1=A, 2=B, 3=C, etc.)*

$\overline{20}$ $\overline{8}$ $\overline{5}$   $\overline{12}$ $\overline{15}$ $\overline{22}$ $\overline{5}$   $\overline{15}$ $\overline{6}$   $\overline{7}$ $\overline{15}$ $\overline{4}$

$\overline{9}$ $\overline{14}$   $\overline{3}$ $\overline{8}$ $\overline{18}$ $\overline{9}$ $\overline{19}$ $\overline{20}$   $\overline{10}$ $\overline{5}$ $\overline{19}$ $\overline{21}$ $\overline{19}$

$\overline{6}$ $\overline{15}$ $\overline{18}$   $\overline{13}$ $\overline{5}$

8. What have you learned from God's Word about how He will turn evil into good in your life?

_____

**Prayer**

1. Thank God for the various ways you have learned from Joseph's life about God turning evil into good.
2. Thank God for the conclusion of the study on Joseph's life and all He has taught you through it.
3. Thank God for the love He has for you in Christ to always turn evil into good in your life.
4. Pray that all you have learned will not be in vain but will be fruitful in your life to increase your knowledge of God and help you to live for Him.

# Curriculums

**BELIEVE IN JESUS Curriculum**

Preschool Teacher's Manual

Preschool Activity Book

Teacher's Manual

Junior Activity Book

Senior Activity Book


**LIVING FOR GOD Curriculum**

Preschool Teacher's Manual

Preschool Activity Book

Teacher's Manual

Junior Activity Book

Senior Activity Book


**GROW IN LIVING FOR GOD Curriculum**

Teacher's Manual

Junior Activity Book

Senior Activity Book


**BIBLE STUDY ON JOSEPH (For Older Children & Youth)**

Leader's Guide

Student Workbook


These curriculums are available in digital and print versions.

For print and eBook purchase: Amazon.com and other retail outlets.

For digital PDF download: www.setapartchild.com.

# About The Author

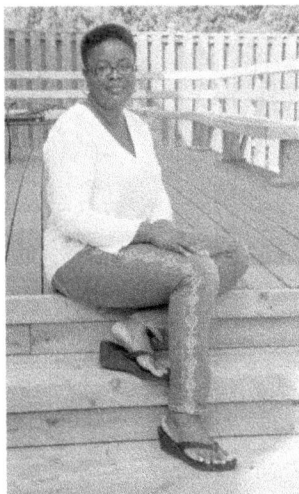

Bisi Adeyi is more than anything else a Christian who loves the Lord.

She has a calling to minister to children and children's ministry teachers which God blesses and equips her for. Her children's ministry experience which started in 1985 includes teaching children of all age-groups, organizing summer camps and Bible clubs, speaking at children's conferences and programs, coordinating children's ministry department in churches, and training children's ministry teachers.

She writes exciting Bible-based curriculums & resources to teach children to know and live for God daily. The resources include Bible studies, devotionals, tracts, newsletters and articles. Empowered by the Holy Spirit's revelation to her on John 17:17, she ministers to children to be set apart by the truth of God's Word to live for Him. By the grace of God, her heart's desire through her writings is to birth and nurture the *set apart child*.

In addition to writing and children's ministry, Bisi enjoys reading, making memories with her family, batch cooking, hosting people in her home, sewing and personal events planning. She is married to her best friend and together they have two young adult children.

For more information about her and what she believes, please go on her website at www.setapartchild.com.

www.ingramcontent.com/pod-product-compliance
Lightning Source LLC
Chambersburg PA
CBHW081226020426
42331CB00012B/3084